A Cluster of
LIMERICKS

David J. Catchpoole

Zafferona Press

Published by Zafferona Press

ISBN-13: 978-0-9953943-1-5
1. Poetry 2. Humour
Cover design by Satori

This book is dedicated to the Frog in the Kettle.

Contents

The Spry Sailor

There was a spry sailor from Cuba,

Who loved to play tunes on his tuba;

But when the wind roared,

He fell overboard,

So his tuba he used as a scuba.

The Rhea

A rhea from South Korea,

While filling its glass with sangria,

Thought "I can stop drinking,

But how to stop thinking?

I really have no idea…"

The Bishop of Germany

There was an old bishop of Germany,

Whose church was leaky and verminy;

He preached how to preen,

For moral hygiene,

But the rodents all thought him too sermony.

The Sweet Thief

A thief when picking a pocket,

Never took money, just chocolate;

Although uncontrite,

He was very polite,

Invariably leaving a docket.

The Mayor of Madrid

The austere mayor of Madrid,

Said "Circuses I forbid!"

The tumblers and clowns,

Pursued him with frowns,

So under the big top he hid.

The Tarantula

There was a ranchero called Santo,

Whose tarantula learnt Esperanto;

He taught it to rhyme,

And in a short time,

It finished its seventeenth canto.

The Lady from Timbuktu

A lady from Timbuktu,

Was dining on vindaloo;

The waiter asked,

"How is your repast?"

She replied, "Oh, tickety-boo!"

The Azalea

A flower-show entrant of Australia,

Was perfecting his purebred azalea;

But the more he coerced it

To try to come first, it

Only felt droopier and snailier.

The Geologist

A geologist named Theresa,

Ventured too close to a geyser;

With a head full of steam,

(And disquiet extreme)

She ran home and sat in the freezer.

The Prince's Parcel

An unpopular prince in a castle,

Received a dangerous parcel;

He unwrapped a drama,

And said (now much calmer) -

"It'll hurt me much less than a farce'll."

The Taste-Tester

A royal taste-tester from Hastings,

Dreaded each one of his tastings;

For when he collapsed,

The whole meal was scrapped;

He just couldn't stand such wastings.

The Panacea

A miracle cure injected,

Was endorsed by folks resurrected;

But sales declined,

When a zombie whined,

"Use only as directed!"

The Frog in the Kettle

There once was a frog in a kettle,

Whose stomach refused to settle;

But even when boiled,

The frog was not foiled,

For it had such steely mettle.

The Mathematician

A mathematician called May,

Designed a fine disarray,

With columns and rows,

Where anything goes,

And a formula to disobey.

The Boy of the North Pole

There was a boy of the North Pole,

To travel south was his goal;

But he couldn't work out,

Which way was south,

So he ended up digging a hole.

The Painter from Ulladulla

A painter from Ulladulla,

Yearned for an alien colour;

To her delight,

A meteorite,

Bestowed it with help from her muller.

The New Masseuse

A novice masseuse called Miss Hoyle,

Applied her virgin oil;

She loved to soothe,

Her rubs were smooth,

Until she touched the boil.

The Apatosaurus

An arthritic apatosaurus,

Found in a tattered thesaurus,

His old distinction,

Which'd suffered extinction -

The regal "brontosaurus".

The Girl from Fiji

There once was a girl from Fiji,

Who went to a jamboree;

That night there were present,

Many a gallant,

But her heart was an absentee.

The Ghoul of the Marsh

There once was a ghoul of the marsh,

Whose flak was particularly harsh;

In their graves the bards turned,

When their epics were spurned,

And they haunted that ghoul of the marsh.

The Ailing Soprano

A soprano asked from her insurer,

Compensation for coloratura;

He answered "No deal,

But I'm sure you will heal."

She emerged from the meeting demurer.

The Chubby Soldier

A chubby soldier from Perth,

Was expelled on account of his girth;

By the close of the fray,

He was thin as a rake,

Due to cibarian dearth.

The Backpacker

A backpacker from the equator,

Screamed at an alligator;

It couldn't be beaten,

She thought she'd be eaten...

"It's a model," said the curator.

The Cadaver's Dream

A cadaver began to convulse,

For he dreamt that he still had a pulse;

He awoke in frustration,

But to his consolation,

He found it was perfectly false.

The Jock of Gibraltar

A jumpy, young jock of Gibraltar,

Was a marathon somersaulter;

Jibes made him stronger

(For those he'd go longer);

Only the cheers made him falter.

The Therapist

There once was a therapist called Dora,

Whose gentle, soothing aura,

Helped her relax

Insomniacs,

'Till she became a snorer.

The Review

A literate cat who was smitten,

Sent a love letter she'd written;

Her beau's reply "Litter!"

Misconstrued made her bitter;

He just wished to sire her kitten.

The Tourist from Jupiter

There once was a tourist from Jupiter,

Whose travels kept making him stupider;

"It's narrowed my mind!

Should've stayed behind,

For the telly's far better on Jupiter."

The Friend

In a world of propaganda,

Where people freely slander,

Just one friend

Will buck the trend;

He'll go to jail for candour.

The Mermaid Hunter

A mermaid hunter called Nester,

Whom skeptics and vampires would pester;

Escaped their spleen,

In his submarine

But from mermen he couldn't sequester.

The Farmer of Scandinavia

A farmer of Scandinavia,

Wished for his lunch to be gravier;

So he dipped in a trough,

His beef stroganoff,

Dampening his cows' behaviour.

Mr. Lour

A no-nonsense poet named Lour

Was as dour as he was sour;

But eating a chilli,

He promptly went silly,

And tickled his toes with a flower.

The Inventor's New Shemozzle

An inventor got in a shemozzle,

Upgrading his slimeblaster's nozzle;

"It just won't fire

The way I require."

Said his dog - "Perhaps your schnozz'll."

The Time Traveller

A time traveller from the future,

Needed to have a suture;

The stitch in time

Was so sublime,

That she became a moocher.

The Builder

An overworked builder was fired,

Simply because he'd expired;

He sighed and said,

"I'm not quite dead…

I'm just tremendously tired."

The Ornithorhynchus

In our pond lives an ornithorhynchus,

With electroreceptors that plink us;

We've every intention,

To escape its attention;

For those venomous spurs could just sink us.

The Impoverished Poet

An impoverished poet of Helsinki,

Bewailed that his sleeves were all inky;

The stains were indelible,

His refrains just weren't sellable,

And his typewriter was real rinky-dinky.

The Antiphony

Sandra, Marlene and Tiffany,

Laced their Christmas antiphony,

With pert innuendo,

And at the crescendo,

Their headmaster had an epiphany.

The Tourist from Andorra

A debonair tourist from Andorra,

Fell in love with a señora;

He showed her Madagascar,

Then made (in Alaska)

A proposal beneath an aurora.

The Warning

A sorrowful, falling supernal

Cautioned a rising infernal:

"Always remember

Your every last ember!"

"- I will; I kept a damned journal!"

The Tsetse

The friend and colleague of Betsy,

Was a loyal, industrious tsetse;

It did accrue

Yuppie flu,

She took it, therefore, to the vetsy.

The Reformed Iguana

There was a reformed iguana,

Who daily practised dhyana;

With each incarnation,

Away from tarnation,

She clambered towards nirvana.

The Graphic Designer

A graphic designer from Togo,

Travelled to work on his pogo;

Without any cares,

He bounced upstairs,

And bevelled a company logo.

The Old Gnome

There was an old gnome in a garden,

Whose Phrygian cap did harden;

Said the spouse, "You've gone rigid!

But I thought you were frigid…

Good gracious, I do beg your pardon."

The MC from Congo

A charming MC from Congo,

Wrote lyrics in rongorongo;

To make well heard,

Each picture-word,

He rapped on a fabulous bongo.

The Jolly Jester

There once was a jolly, old jester,

In whom ennui did fester;

The gloom was bewitchin',

But he trudged to the kitchen,

And cured his ennui with a zester.

The Word-Eater

A word-eater called Mrs. Powell,

Relished each consonant and vowel;

Whatever the venue,

She plundered the menu,

Then wiped her gob with a towel.

The Restoration

I'm Hope and this is Eustace,

The land we love produced us;

We were displaced,

All but effaced;

An ecologist reintroduced us.

The Urchin of China

An obliging, proud urchin of China,

Worked as a horseshoe-shiner;

While he waxed,

The horse relaxed

On a fine, equine recliner.

The Young Lady of Russia

There was a young lady of Russia,

Who landed a job as an usher;

She used to get by,

By cleaning a sty,

But the theatre, she found, was plusher.

The Radiolaria

There once were some radiolaria,

Whose conduct and form became lairier;

They drank and mutated,

Till intoxicated;

They played rock 'n' roll and got hairier.

The Man from Samoa

There once was a man from Samoa,

Who raced and won as a rower;

With laurel's dearth,

They marked his worth,

By giving him a pink feather boa.

The Word-Builder of Babel

There was a word-builder of Babel,

Who questioned the worth of a label;

It's core imprecision,

Gave her some vision -

Language itself is a fable.

The Jacaranda

To mark his first philander,

George planted a jacaranda;

It started to wilt,

Then at full tilt,

It crashed onto his veranda.

The Welsh Scientist

An equable scientist of Wales,

Longed to get all the details;

Then one day, aghast,

He discovered the last,

And completely went off the rails.

Ray

There was a child actor, Ray Hughes,

Whose autograph signings made news;

But when fully grown,

He was left all alone,

So he often missed his queues.

The Entrepreneur of Gondwana

An entrepreneur of Gondwana,

Puzzled to build a cabana;

It couldn't be solved,

For he wasn't evolved,

With a brain smaller than a sultana.

The Tamer

A tamer of the Himalayas,

Boldly defied the naysayers;

He cooked some spaghetti,

To lure the Yeti,

But soon he was saying his prayers.

The Bones

An archaeologist called Jones,

Found radio-active bones;

Each one had clumps,

Of numbered bumps,

Caused by mobile phones.

The Punk Rocker Down Under

There was a punk rocker down under,

Who moshed in a massive rotunda;

Its dome was designed,

With volume in mind,

And a funnel to capture the thunder.

A Dieting Tip

For people who want to get thinner,

Spaghettification's a winner;

Memories bedizen

The event horizon,

And the black hole loves a long dinner.

The Strict Man

There was a strict man of Romania,

Whose Labrador kept getting brainier;

It studied psychology,

And microbiology,

Then cured the man of leash-mania.

The Thief of Brazil

An exuberant thief of Brazil,

Would dance the mobster quadrille;

He'd shuffle and flail,

And tread on your tail,

Then mug you just for the thrill.

The Wedding Knell

Cindy, the bride of a welder

Was ardent when first he beheld 'er;

But while he soldered,

Her apathy smouldered;

Because she'd gone out he expelled 'er.

The Young Dragon

A young dragon's life is full

Of fun with a ball of wool;

But when all entangled,

He just can't be wrangled;

Chaos the strings will pull.

The Hidebound Shepherd

A hidebound, old shepherd with a crook,

Located his black sheep forsook;

Said the sheep - "I'm a goth,

So, man of the cloth,

Perhaps you should try a new look."

The Corpse

A corpse who had lived on the pension,

Requested a little extension;

The clerk malfunctioned

At such presumption;

It went against every convention.

The Glazier

The panes of an urban glazier,

Got hazier and hazier;

He tried each soap,

With fading hope,

Till at last he applied euphrasia.

The Lady with Gills

There is a strange lady with gills,

Through which she sings beautiful trills;

For every performance,

She garners great plaudits,

And then the media grills.

The Kendo Panda

There once was a kendo panda,

Whose bearing couldn't be grander;

It swashed the bamboo,

At the Forest Tattoo;

'Twas invested as Knight Commander.

The Puzzler of Laos

There was a fraught puzzler of Laos,

Who fled from the riddle of chaos;

In a tranquil pagoda,

He met a decoder,

Who said, "For this crypt use your naos."

The Rock Climber

A dashing, rock-climbing Mister,

Developed a horrible blister;

Although he was tough,

He got in a huff,

For it marred his spectacular vista.

The Chef of Victoria

There was a grand chef of Victoria,

Whose ice-cream gave people euphoria;

Their taste-buds smiled,

Fully beguiled,

By its flavoursome phantasmagoria.

The Biography

Of a trailblazer there's a biography,

But her name has capricious orthography;

At times it goes bargin'

Right over the margin,

Upsettin' the tidy typography.

The Explorer

An explorer went into a jungle,

And emerged with a lurgy most fungal;

To bathe and romp,

In a putrid swamp,

Apparently was a slight bungle.

The Party Planner

A party planner called Quincy,

Was quite allergic to tinsey;

He tried his most,

To please each host,

But his face was frequently wincy.

The Atheist Ant

An atheist ant of Atlantis,

Questioned the news of a mantis:

"You say doom is nigh,

But how, where and why?

Pray don't be a damn obscurantist!"

The Botanist

A botanist called Beryl Bardon,

Grew a carnivorous garden;

It devoured ten souls,

But seven were trolls,

So Beryl received a pardon.

The Great Fool of Antiquity

There was a great fool of antiquity,

Who strove against iniquity;

Despite the jeers,

His bold ideas,

Have since attained ubiquity.

The Tumbler from Anatolia

A tumbler from Anatolia,

Yearned to become much rollier;

A spiral logistic,

From a whirling, great mystic,

Helped him get rollier and holier.

The Publican

A wonderful sir is the publican,

His till can hold more than a bubblican;

He'll sure entertain us,

And gently restrain us;

He'll gladly go to all the troublican.

The Employer at the Cove

An employer held sway at a cove;

On illegal immigrants he throve;

He worked them for ages,

On miniscule wages,

Then finally, he himself shrove.

The Professor

There lived a respected professor,

Who was an immaculate dresser;

He favoured cravats,

Over bare facts,

And was rudely exposed as a guesser.

The Politician from Lydia

A sly politician from Lydia,

Made his constituents giddier,

By hiring some pipers,

To hypnotize vipers,

Thus winning the seat of Ophidia.

The Inventor from Argentina

An inventor from Argentina,

Desired to get much leaner;

So she shrank her fruit,

Till it was minute,

And her eyesight got much keener.

The Detective

An overzealous detective,

Found his donut defective;

He arrested the baker

(A real troublemaker)

And decreed a confective corrective.

The Pilot

A witty chiquita called Violet,

Played as a skywriting pilot;

Her words of derision,

Had such precision,

She could strike the smallest bullseyelet.

The Violin

A jaded, glum violin,

Repulsed by its own inane din,

Shed its strings,

And worldly things,

Then sought the timbre within.

The Restaurateur of Jamaica

A restaurateur of Jamaica,

Enchanted each holidaymaker,

With maritime décor,

Delectable crayslaw,

And cutlery handles of nacre.

The Damsel of Camelot

A sun-loving damsel of Camelot,

Swooned at the news of her nanobot:

"I warn thee, my cutie,

('Tis my medical duty) -

That mole be not just a beauty spot."

The Bug-Fixer

A bug-fixer up in Vienna,

Repaired a shoddy antenna;

He asked "You receiving?"

Said the bug (disbelieving) -

"I'm picking up Radio Gehenna!"

The Neurotic from Nowhere

There was a neurotic from Nowhere,

Who sported a white wig of mohair;

She combed it all day,

Her fears to allay,

Until the wig finally had no hair.

The Poet from Munster

To a lunch went a poet from Munster,

Who fancied himself a funster;

But his verse super-sillious,

Made the host bilious;

She treated that terrible punster.

Jazmyrelda

A matchmaker called Jazmyrelda,

Was quite an accomplished melder;

But now she's divorced,

For her marriage was forced,

And her husband always misspelled 'er.

The American Skeptic

A skeptic who lived in America,

Examined occult esoterica;

In a mystic acrostic,

Was the name of a gnostic -

His future fiancée, called Erica.

The Contractor

A contractor who worked in Algeria,

Thought his life couldn't be drearier;

Without any hope,

He just couldn't cope,

But then he contracted diphtheria.

McFeasel

A rugged, old painter, McFeasel,

Drove a motorized easel;

He crossed all soils,

On a full tank of oils;

And painted his landscapes with diesel.

The Mongolian Maiden

A maiden who lived in Mongolia,

Wore in her hair a magnolia;

The allure and the smell,

Of the bloom and the belle

Cured all mankind of melancholia

(Briefly).

The Punctilious Pirate

A pirate who sailed under Pisces,

Made of all ships on the high seas,

Keen investigations,

And if regulations,

Were flouted he brought on great crises.

The Boy from Mozambique

A boy from Mozambique,

Was playing hide-and-seek;

He found all his friends

With his GPS;

He must've been some kind of geek.

The Lumberjack

A burly, great lumberjack, Pinter,

Was crushed by a redwood one winter,

His friends knelt to pray,

But then heard him say -

"Relax, it's only a splinter!"

Heat

There once was a rusty gasfitter,

Who got the hots for a frayed knitter;

Between pipes and wool

Their fervour was full;

Their weather never was bitter.

The Insomniac

An insomniac of the Bahamas,

Went to the zoo in pyjamas;

The counting of sheep,

Had not helped him sleep,

So he'd got a prescription for llamas.

www.ingramcontent.com/pod-product-compliance
Lightning Source LLC
Chambersburg PA
CBHW020521030426
42337CB00011B/492

* 9 7 8 0 9 9 5 3 9 4 3 1 5 *